COMPOSERS SHO

Original Compositions by Outstanding Composers

BOOK 3

Intermediate

Contents

for Dr. Kevin Caldwell and Cindy Caldwell

Safari Stampede

Kevin Costley

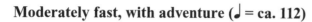

Moderately fast, with adventure (♩ = ca. 112)

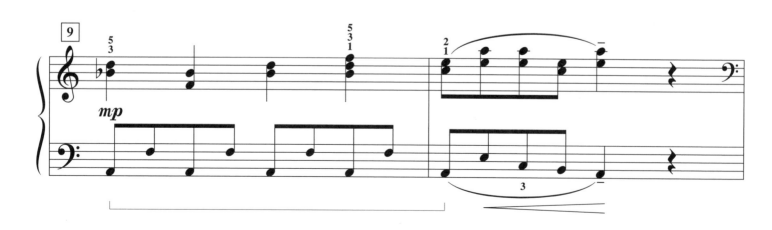

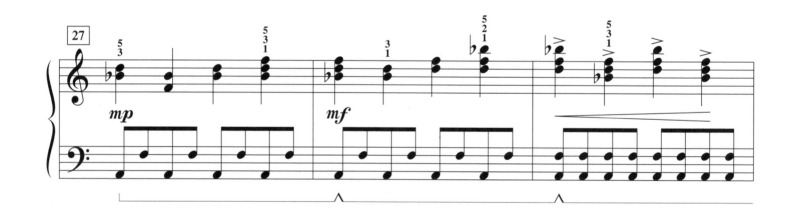

Castles in the Sand

Majestic castles in the sand
stand tall for half a day,
Until the rushing tide sweeps in
and washes them away.

Judith R. Strickland

The Proud Prince

Loretta Pritchard

10

The (Almost) Late for School Toccata

Pat Boozer

14

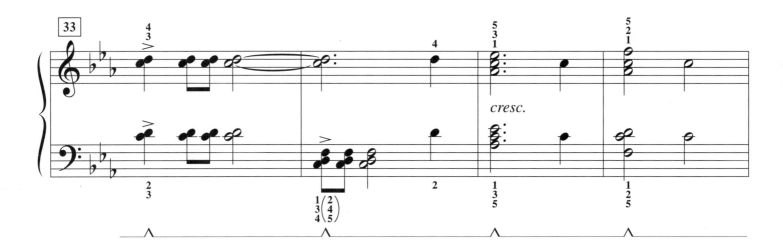

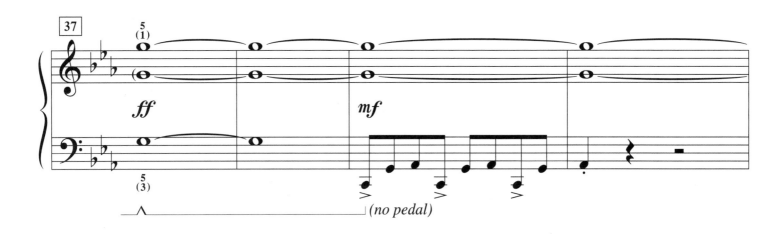

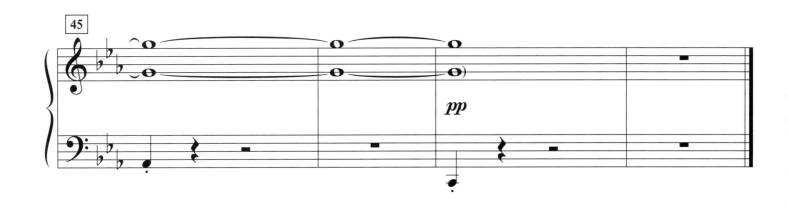

FF1356

Needle in the Hay

Rebecca A. Pulju

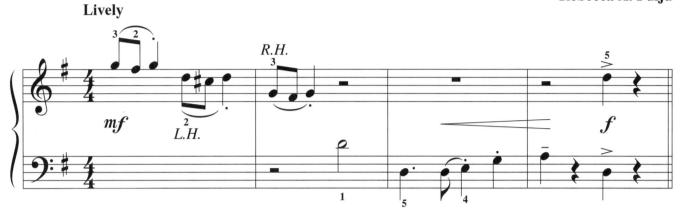

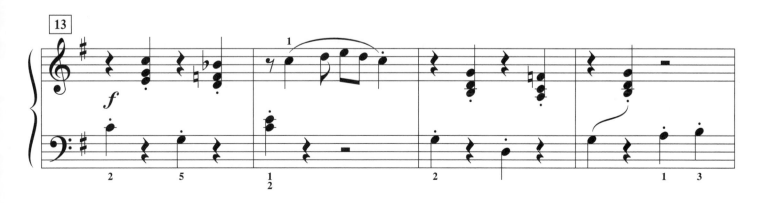

16

FF1356

Yes!

Pat Boozer

20

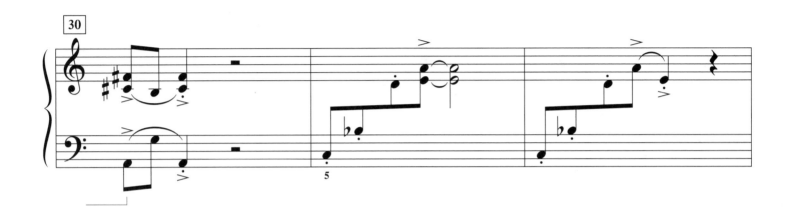

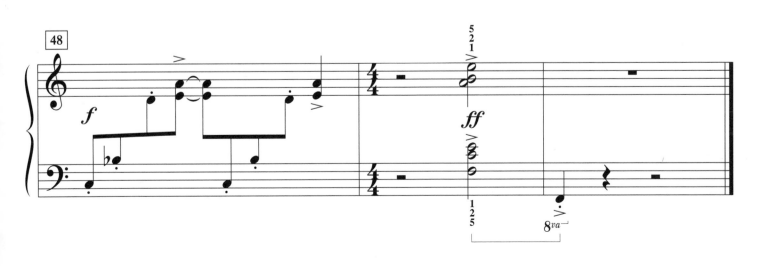

Valse Élégance

Beatrice A. Miller

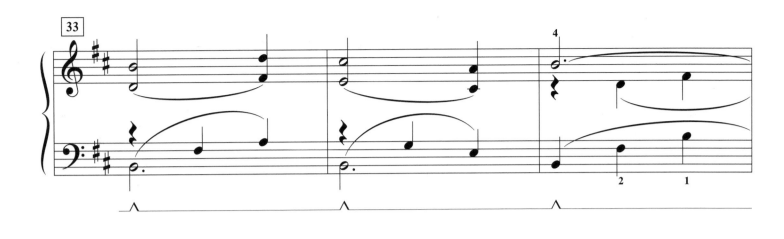

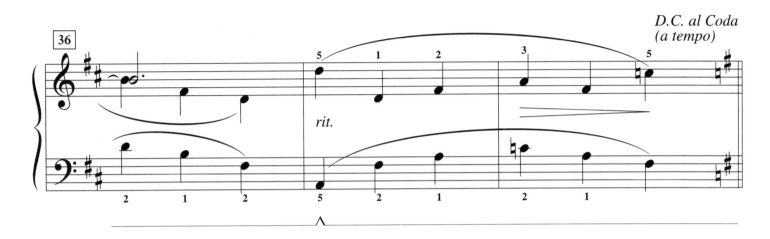

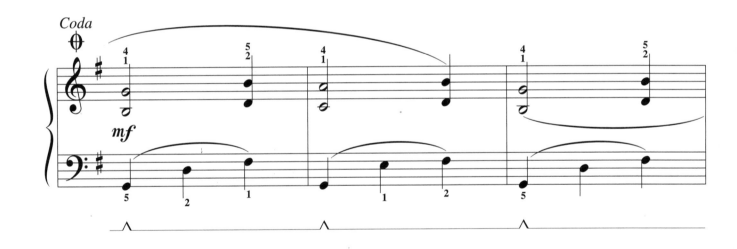

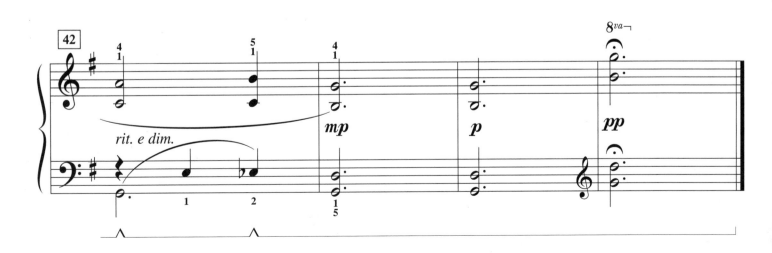